First Facts®

Transportation Zone

Semitrucks

in Action

by Lola M. Schaefer

CAPSTONE PRESS
a capstone imprint

First Facts is published by Capstone Press,
151 Good Counsel Drive, P.O. Box 669, Mankato, Minnesota 56002.
www.capstonepub.com

Books published by Capstone Press are manufactured with paper
containing at least 10 percent post-consumer waste.

Library of Congress Cataloging-in-Publication Data
Schaefer, Lola M., 1950–
  Semitrucks in action/by Lola M. Schaefer.
      p. cm.—(First facts. Transportation zone)
  Includes bibliographical references and index.
  Summary: "Discusses the history, function, and workings of semitrucks"—Provided
by publisher.
  ISBN 978-1-4296-6826-2 (library binding)
  1. Tractor trailer combinations—Juvenile literature. I. Title.
  TL230.15.S328 2012
  629.224—dc22   2010054618

Editorial Credits
Karen L. Daas and Anthony Wacholtz, editors; Gene Bentdahl, designer; Eric Gohl,
      media researcher; Laura Manthe, production specialist

Image Credits
Capstone Studio/Karon Dubke, 10, 14, 17, 22
Getty Images Inc./Buyenlarge, 6, 9
iStockphoto/Wendell and Carolyn, 18
Shutterstock/Cheryl Ann Quigley, cover; Christian Lagerek, 1; Fernando
  Rodrigues, 21; Henryk Sadura, 13; Mike Flippo, 5, Timothy Epp, 17 (inset)

Printed in the United States of America in North Mankato, Minnesota.
032011   006110CGF11

Table of Contents

Semitrucks

With a rumble and a roar, semitrucks take to the highway. Semitrucks are large trucks. Semis move **cargo** from one place to another. These trucks often carry large, heavy loads and travel long distances.

cargo: goods that are carried from one place to another

6

Before Semitrucks

People used trucks and trains to carry cargo before semitrucks were invented. But trucks could not carry very large, heavy loads. Trains could only deliver cargo to train stops.

Early Semitrucks

   The earliest semitrucks were trucks and wagons. People attached wagons to the backs of trucks. These semis could not carry much cargo. Some trucks did not have cabs. The driver sat on a seat above a small fuel tank.

9

exhaust pipe

cab

fifth wheel

fuel tank

Parts of a Tractor

Semitrucks have two main parts, the tractor and the trailer. The tractor has many parts. The engine is under the hood. A fuel tank is on one or both sides of the cab. Hot gases from the engine come out of exhaust pipe. A metal plate on the back of the tractor is called the fifth wheel. A tractor has six to 10 tires.

FREIGHTLINER

Parts of a Trailer

A semitruck's trailer holds cargo. A trailer has a **kingpin** and landing gear. The kingpin works with the fifth wheel to lock the trailer to the tractor. Landing gear supports the trailer's front when it's not locked to the tractor. Trailers have four to eight tires.

kingpin: a metal rod used to join a trailer to a tractor

kingpin

landing gear

tires

23

13

engine

How Semis Work

The driver attaches the tractor to a trailer. The tractor pulls the trailer. The tractor has a large diesel engine. Diesel fuel powers the engine. Power from the engine turns the tractor's tires.

Driving a Semitruck

Drivers sit in the tractor cab. They use a steering wheel, pedals, and levers to drive the tractor. Drivers pick up and unload cargo at a loading dock. They keep a **log** of their time on the road and the distance they traveled. Some drivers use an electronic logbook to log their time.

log: a written record; semitruck drivers keep a log of the time and distance of each trip

electronic logbook

Semitrucks Today

Semitrucks today move many kinds of cargo. They carry items such as books and clothing. Some trailers are kept cold so they can carry fresh food or flowers. Livestock trailers deliver animals. Tank trailers hold liquids. Flatbed trailers carry large, heavy machinery. Rain or shine, semis travel across the country to deliver their loads.

Semitruck Facts

- Some semitrucks have more than one trailer. A second trailer can be joined to the back of the first trailer.

- People attend driving schools to become semitruck drivers. Students train for eight to 12 weeks. They study and practice driving for about 500 hours.

- A full tanker trailer can hold as much liquid as 200 bathtubs.

- The fuel tanks on some tractors can hold almost 300 gallons (1,100 liters) of fuel.

In the United States semis carry about 11 billion tons (10 billion metric tons) of cargo each year.

Hands On: Momentum

Semitrucks take longer to stop than cars because semis have more momentum. Momentum is the force an object has when it is moving. All moving objects have momentum.

What You Need

ruler
dime
quarter

What You Do

1. Place the ruler flat on a table.
2. Place the dime on the table at one end of the ruler.
3. Place the quarter behind the dime. Flick the quarter into the dime. Using the ruler, note how far the dime moves.
4. Place the quarter at the same end of the ruler. Place the dime behind the quarter.
5. Flick the dime into the quarter. Note how far the quarter moves. The quarter moves less than the dime moved.

Both moving coins have momentum. The quarter moves the dime farther because the quarter has more momentum. At the same speed, heavier objects have more momentum than lighter objects. Semis have more momentum because they are heavier than cars.

Glossary

cargo (KAR-goh)—goods that are carried from one place to another

diesel fuel (DEE-zuhl FYOO-uhl)—a heavy fuel that burns to make power; semitrucks run on diesel fuel

exhaust (eg-ZAWST)—the waste gases produced by the engine of a motor vehicle

kingpin (KING-pin)—a metal rod used to join a trailer to a tractor

log (LOG)—a written record; semitruck drivers keep a log of the time and distance of each trip

Read More

Doeden, Matt. *Semitrucks*. Mighty Machines. Mankato, Minn.: Capstone Press, 2007.

Ransom, Candice. *Big Rigs on the Move*. Vroom-Vroom. Minneapolis: Lerner Publications Group, 2011.

Internet Sites

FactHound offers a safe, fun way to find Internet sites related to this book. All of the sites on FactHound have been researched by our staff.

Here's all you do:

Visit *www.facthound.com*

Type in this code: 9781429668262

 Super-cool stuff! Check out projects, games and lots more at **www.capstonekids.com**

Index